She is Strong

Women Leaders of the Bible

Mark Sundy

She is Strong and Graceful
Women Leaders of the Bible
By Mark Sundy

© 2017 Mark Sundy

Printed in the United States of America

Dedication

This book is dedicated to all the Mary's in my family history. All past, present, and future generations. My family, all Protestants, have a history of giving respect and honor to Mary the mother of Jesus for over two hundred years by naming some of their children after her. To my mother, Mary Pauline Harrell Sundy, 1929-2002. To my future granddaughter, Mary Eleanor Sundy Benton. My daughter has already picked this name for her future daughter. To my great grandmother, Mary Loutista Gray Harrell, 1861-1948. To my other great grandmother, Mary Ann Maher Hart, 1857-1939. To a great aunt of six generations ago, Mary Ann Wallingsford, 1816-1881. And of course to Mary the mother of Jesus.

I would also like to dedicate this book to my newest grandson, Hunter Allen Sundy, who is due to be born in 3 months on December 25, 2017.

Acknowledgements

I am grateful to my daughter, Kristina Sundy Benton, and my son, Nathan Sundy, who make life a joy. To my two grandchildren, Hailey and Patton, who are my sunshine. To my father, Allen Sundy, and my mother, Mary Harrell Sundy, who were an inspiration to me. To Samantha Sundy, Gary Faulkner, Beverly Sundy, and Linda Sundy for their support.

I am grateful to the Father, the Son, and the Holy Spirit, the one and only true God—the Blessed Trinity for giving me the breath of life.

I also express gratitude and appreciation to Randy Chandler and Prophetic Grace Network for the prophetic word "publishing" which motivated me to finish the book that I had started six years earlier and to start publishing other books.

I would like to thank my sister, Rita Sundy Faulkner, for her caring support while I was working on this book.

I would also like to thank my two brothers, Randall Sundy and Steve Sundy, for their encouragement.

I would like to extend gratitude to Henry and Mary, Howard and Carolyn, Ralph and Jessica, Brenda and Steve, Freddy, Lou and Corina, Kathy and Arturo, Lupe, and Jacque for their prayers, grace, and loving compassion.

I owe my gratitude to a multitude of Christian Mentors, Teachers, Pastors, Prophets, Evangelists, and Sunday School Teachers who helped me in my walk with the Lord Jesus Christ.

Table of Contents

Introduction

Women Leaders of the Bible

__She is strong and graceful__, as well as cheerful about the future. (Proverbs 31:25, CEV, emphasis added)

There were many godly women leaders in the Old and New Testament of the Bible who were strong, graceful, and cheerful about the future. These leaders include Deborah the prophet and judge, Abigail a woman of good understanding (wise), Mary the mother of Jesus, Phoebe the Deacon, Esther the Queen that saved her people, Tabitha full of good works, and Eve the mother of all living.

Though gender is differentiated in the Bible as prophet and prophetess, deacon and deaconess, and prince and princess, the responsibilities of the office are the same regardless of whether the occupant is male or female.

The women leaders we will study show many godly traits the Woman of God must emulate.

Prayer: *Heavenly Father, I come humbly before Your throne of grace and ask You to help me in fulfilling my destiny as a Woman of God. Help me to fulfill all of Your plans for my life. Grant me strength, humility, and wisdom. Fill me to overflowing with Your Holy Spirit, in Jesus' name, I pray. Amen!*

Chapter 1

Deborah the Prophet and Judge

In the midst of the violent and turbulent aftermath of Joshua's conquest of Canaan, "the Lord raised up judges" to provide leadership for the kingless people (Judges 2:16). Deborah was an Old Testament prophet and judge over Israel. Her story takes place in chapters four and five of the book of Judges. Deborah was married and was the wife of Lapidoth. The Jewish culture at the time would have required Deborah to submit to her husband as the leader, provider, and protector of their household. Then she would go to "work" each morning as the political leader of Israel, their prophet and judge. Deborah would sit under a palm tree between Ramah and Bethel in the mountains of Ephraim. The children of Israel would come to her there for judgment.

She was a woman of integrity and devotion to God. As a prophet, she received divine revelation and as a judge she arbitrated legal disputes.

In Judges 4:6-7, Deborah told Barak he was called by God to take a 10,000 man army against Sisera who was invading Israel's territory. She told him God would deliver Sisera into his hand. However, Barak did not receive God's call with courage and enthusiasm, but set a condition on his "obedience".

> And Barak said to her, "If you will go with me, then I will go; but if you will not go with me, I will not go!" (Judges 4:8 NKJV)

Deborah and Barak went to battle against Sisera and his troops. Sisera's army was defeated, but Barak did not get the glory. Sisera was actually killed by another woman named Jael. When he went into her tent to rest, Jael took a tent peg and hammer and drove the tent peg through his temple.

Deborah's prophecy was fulfilled. Deborah's courage and leadership had led the nation of Israel to victory in spite of Barak's hesitation to be obedient to God's call. "The Song of Deborah" in Judges 5:1-31, records the battle and was used as a victory hymn and a guide to future kings and leaders of Israel.

In her role as a prophet and judge over Israel, she was the political head of that nation. In today's time that would've been the equivalent of Margaret Thatcher as the Prime Minister of the United Kingdom or Golda Meir as the Prime Minister of Israel.

Women Leaders of the Modern Era

According to Wikipedia, Margaret Thatcher was Prime Minister of the United Kingdom from 1979 to 1990. She was the first woman to hold that office and was the longest serving British Prime Minister of the twentieth century. She was nicknamed "The Iron Lady" because of her uncompromising politics and style of leadership. She is known as one of the greatest British politicians.

Golda Meir was the first woman Prime Minister of Israel, according to Wikipedia. She was Prime Minister of Israel from 1969 to 1974. She was also called "The Iron Lady" before that title was given to Margaret Thatcher. She was known as the strong-willed, grey-headed grandmother of Israel. She was in office during the Yom Kippur War.

Prayer: *Heavenly Father, I come humbly before Your throne of grace and ask You to teach me to be the leader you have called me to be. Teach me to be the Woman of God I should be. Help me to be a humble but strong leader, in Jesus' name, I pray. Amen!*

Chapter 2

Abigail a Woman of Good Understanding (Wise)

*The name of the man was Nabal, and the name of his wife Abigail. **And she was a woman of good understanding and beautiful appearance**; but the man was harsh and evil in his doings.* (1 Samuel 25:3, NKJV, emphasis added)

Abigail was married to a very rich man named Nabal. He owned three thousand sheep and one thousand goats, but he lacked wisdom and understanding. He was harsh and evil. In fact, his name, Nabal, means "fool."

Abigail was very beautiful and her wisdom and understanding saved the lives of her husband and his servants.

Nabal had his men shearing his sheep when David entered the picture. David sent ten young men to ask for food from him. Nabal basically said, "Who does this David think he is?" Then he foolishly, refused to give any food to David's men.

When David heard about this, he gathered his army to attack Nabal and his household. David's plan was not to leave one male alive of all who belong to the house of Nabal.

When Abigail was told how foolishly her husband acted, she anticipated what might result from his actions. She made haste and took food to David and his men. Abigail seized the information given, understood what needed to be done, and then did it.

When Abigail saw David, she dismounted quickly from her donkey and fell facedown and bowed to the ground before him. She asked for forgiveness for foolish Nabal and his household.

Abigail's plea brought an immediate positive response from David. We see David's instant gratitude, first to God and then to Abigail. David recognizes the hand of God in this situation. He praises this wise woman for taking action to stop him from causing innocent bloodshed. Except for her intervention, the obliteration of Nabal and his household would surely have been the result. She stood in the gap protecting both parties.

David said to Abigail, "Blessed is the Lord God of Israel who sent you this day to me, and blessed is your advice as you have kept me this day from coming to bloodshed and from avenging myself with my own hand."

In verse 35, David accepts the provisions from Abigail and instructs her to go home in peace telling her she had nothing to fear from him. David wisely heeds her words and request, choosing to allow God to take care of the situation with her husband.

After ten days, the Lord did indeed take care of foolish Nabal and he died of an apparent heart attack. When David heard of this, he proposed marriage to Abigail and she accepted.

Abigail's life with David would not always be easy. Instead of living in an established home in one location, Abigail becomes part of a group who moved from place to place avoiding the forces of Saul. Abigail was sent by God to help and support David on his journey to the throne.

It is interesting to note that Nabal was a fool, and yet he was still wealthy and rich.

It is very possible his wealth and riches were due in part to Abigail's intervention in his business affairs.

A beautiful woman that also possesses "good understanding" is priceless.

How many men would love to have a wife like Abigail? She was beautiful. She was sensible. She was practical. She had great wisdom and understanding. This is indeed the Abigail Blessing. Proverbs 31:10-31 is a description of a wife whose value is beyond that of the rubies and precious gems. This type of wife is also as rare as a precious gem.

Proverbs 31:11 states, "The heart of her husband safely trusts her; so he will have no lack of gain. She does him good and not evil all the days of her life." The Proverbs 31 wife is described as a rising early to prepare food and make clothes for her household.

Proverbs 31 also states she has good business sense. She considers a field and buys it and from the profits plants a vineyard. Verse 23 states, "Her husband is known in the gates when he sits among the elders of the land."

Proverbs 31:28 also states the rewards of being this type of wife and mother. "Her children rise up and call her blessed; her husband also, and he praises her." Verse 30 says, "Charm is deceitful and beauty is passing, but a woman who fears the Lord, she shall be praised."

This describes the perfect wife. How many wives would fulfill all these qualities? It would seem to be almost impossible. However, it appears Nabal's wife Abigail did have all of these qualities. She was an example of the Proverbs 31 wife. David recognized these qualities in Abigail and knew she would be an asset to him.

It is interesting to note that a woman named Pauline Phillips, who wrote under the pen name, Abigail Van Buren, became a very popular advice columnist. According to Wikipedia, her parents were immigrants from Russia and also were Jewish. So, it is evident that she chose the biblical name Abigail as her pen name because Abigail was noted for being sensible and insightful.

Abigail Van Buren, also known as "Dear Abby," is very well known for her practical advice on a variety of subjects.

David's son Solomon could have learned to be practical and sensible by observing the understanding and wisdom of his step-mother, Abigail.

We all can learn from her and pray for the Abigail Blessing for our lives. Wisdom is a Godly trait and Abigail possessed this trait. Why is wisdom so important, and what does the Bible say about Wisdom?

Wisdom

> *Wisdom is the principal thing; therefore get wisdom. And in all your getting, get understanding.* (Proverbs 4:7 NKJV)

The Cambridge English Dictionary states wisdom is the ability to use your knowledge and experience to make good decisions and judgments. The Oxford English Dictionary defines wisdom as the capacity of judging rightly in matters relating to life.

Charles Haddon Spurgeon defined wisdom as "the right use of knowledge." The Free Dictionary defines wisdom as the ability to discern or judge what is true, right, or lasting; insight; common sense; good judgment.

Wisdom = Knowledge plus Understanding

For the Lord gives skillful and godly Wisdom; from His mouth come knowledge and understanding. (Proverbs 2:6 AMP)

According to the Bible, wisdom is very valuable. It is more valuable than precious and rare gems. It is more valuable than silver and gold. Proverbs 3:15 says, "Wisdom is more precious than rubies; nothing you desire can compare with her" (NLT). Proverbs 16:16 adds, "How much better it is to get wisdom than gold! And to get understanding is to be chosen rather than silver" (NKJV). The Book of Proverbs "personifies" wisdom. "The Lord possessed me at the beginning of his way, before His works of old. I have been established from everlasting, from the beginning, before there was ever an earth" (Proverbs 8:22 NKJV).

A key verse is Proverbs 9:10 tells us, "The [reverent] fear of the Lord [that is, worshiping Him and regarding Him as truly awesome] is the beginning *and* the preeminent part of wisdom [its starting point and its essence], and the knowledge of the Holy One is understanding *and* spiritual insight" (AMP).

Wisdom is practical knowledge and helps us to know how to act and speak in different situations. It gives us the ability to avoid problems as well as the skill to handle those we cannot avoid. However, wisdom goes beyond knowledge and intelligence. The Apostle Paul tells us there is a difference between worldly wisdom and the wisdom from above (see 1 Corinthians 1:18-31). Of course, the source of true wisdom is God.

Those who want wisdom need to enter into a relationship with the One who has all wisdom and wants to give it to His children generously.

James 5:5-8 not only tells us how to seek wisdom, but warns about what will keep us from benefiting from it.

If any of you lacks wisdom, you should ask God, who gives generously to all without finding fault, and it will be given to you. But when you ask, you must believe and not doubt, because the one who doubts is like a wave of the sea, blown and tossed by the wind. That person should not expect to receive anything from the Lord. Such a person is double-minded and unstable in all they do. (NIV)

When God gave Solomon the opportunity to ask for anything he wanted, he chose wisdom above all else.

That night the LORD appeared to Solomon in a dream, and God said, "What do you want? Ask, and I will give it to you!" Solomon replied, "You showed great and faithful love to your servant my father, David, because he was honest and true and faithful to you. And you have continued to show this great and faithful love to him today by giving him a son to sit on his throne. Now, O LORD my God, you have made me king instead of my father, David, but I am like a little child who doesn't know his way around. And here I am in the midst of your own chosen people, a nation so great and numerous they cannot be counted! Give me an understanding heart so that I can govern your people well and know the difference between right and wrong. For who by himself is able to govern this great people of yours?" The Lord was pleased that Solomon had asked for wisdom. So God replied, "Because you have asked for wisdom in governing my people with justice and have not asked for a long life or wealth or the death of your enemies—I will give you what you asked for! I will give you a wise and understanding heart such as no one else has had or ever will have! And I will also give you what you did not ask for—riches and fame! No other king in all the world will be compared to you for the rest of your life! And if you follow me and obey my decrees and my commands as your father, David, did, I will give you a long life. " (1 Kings 3:5-14 NLT)

Solomon wrote of the benefits of wisdom all throughout the book of Proverbs.

Solomon listed the reasons he wrote the Proverbs in 1:2-6.

Their purpose is to teach people wisdom and discipline, to help them understand the insights of the wise. Their purpose is to teach people to live disciplined and successful lives, to help them do what is right, just, and fair. These proverbs will give insight to the simple, knowledge and discernment to the young. Let the wise listen to these proverbs and become even wiser. Let those with understanding receive guidance by exploring the meaning in these proverbs and parables, the words of the wise and their riddles. (NLT)

Proverbs 2:2-3 instructs us to, "Tune your ears to wisdom, and concentrate on understanding. Cry out for insight, and ask for understanding" (NLT).

Pray for Wisdom: *Heavenly Father, I ask You to bestow upon me that which is worth more than gold, silver, and precious gems such as rubies; help me to realize the importance of wisdom. I ask for the godly trait of wisdom, in Jesus' name, Amen!*

Chapter 3

Mary the Mother of Jesus

*And in the sixth month the angel Gabriel was sent from God unto a city of Galilee, named Nazareth, to a virgin espoused to a man whose name was Joseph, of the house of David; and the virgin's name was Mary. And the angel came in unto her, and said**, Hail, thou art highly favored, the Lord is with thee: blessed art thou among women.** And when she saw him, she was troubled at his saying, and cast in her mind what manner of salutation this should be. And the angel said unto her, Fear not, Mary: for thou hast found favor with God. And, behold, thou shalt conceive in thy womb, and bring forth a son, and shalt call his name JESUS. He shall be great, and shall be called the Son of the Highest: and the Lord God shall give unto him the throne of his father David: And he shall reign over the house of Jacob forever; and of his kingdom* *there shall be no end. Then said Mary unto the angel, How shall this be, since I know not a man? And the angel answered and said unto her, the Holy Ghost shall come upon thee, and the power of the Highest shall overshadow thee: therefore also that holy thing which shall be born of thee shall be called the Son of God. And, behold, thy cousin Elizabeth, she hath also conceived a son in her old age: and this is the six month with her, who was called barren.* ***For with God nothing shall be impossible. And Mary said, Behold the handmaid of the Lord; be it unto me according to thy word.*** *And the angel departed from her.* (Luke 1:26-38, KJV, emphasis added))

Mary the mother of Jesus was an extraordinary woman. Mary was highly favored and chosen by God for a special task. She was obedient to God, and she said yes to being the mother of Jesus, God's only son. The Bible does not say much about the childhood of Jesus, but Mary and Joseph were entrusted by God to raise His only Son.

She was overshadowed by the Holy Spirit and Jesus was born by the miracle of a virgin birth. What a monumental task she was given to raise the Son of God. She felt the needles piercing through her heart as she watched the crucifixion of Jesus. Mary was present at Jesus' first recorded miracle at the wedding in Cana.

On the third day there was a wedding in Cana of Galilee, and the mother of Jesus was there. Now both Jesus and His disciples were invited to the wedding. And when they ran out of wine, the mother of Jesus said to Him, "They have no wine." Jesus said to her, "Woman, what does your concern have to do with me? My hour has not yet come. His mother said to the servants, **"Whatever he says to you, do it."** *Now there were set there six water pots of stone, according to the manner of purification of the Jews, containing 20 or 30 gallons apiece. Jesus said to them, "Fill the water pots with water." And they filled them up to the brim. And he said to them, "Draw some out now, and take it to the*

master of the feast." And they took it.
(John 2:1-8 NKJV emphasis added)

Mary had a message for the people then as she does now. That message is **"Whatever he says to you, do it."** Mary's message then and now is to obey Jesus. Obedience to Jesus and His teachings is of paramount importance to all Christians.

Mary is an example of obedience to God, and she possessed the key trait of humility. Just as Moses was the most humble man on Earth in his time, I believe Mary was the most humble person on Earth during her time. I believe she obtained the "favor" of God due to her humility. Why is humility important, and what does the Bible say about humility.

Humility

The sacrifices of God are a broken and contrite heart, O God thou will not despise. (Psalm 51:17 KJV)

Once again it benefits us to learn what God means here in this verse of scripture. What is a broken and contrite heart?

Most of us seldom use the word contrite in our everyday vocabulary. The Merriam-Webster Dictionary defines contrite as a feeling or showing sorrow and **remorse** for a sin or shortcoming.[1] The Amplified Translation of the Bible says, "a contrite heart [broken down with sorrow for sin and humbly and thoroughly penitent]."

Brokenness = broken pride. Contrite = repentant.

Isaiah 57:15 says God inhabits or lives with those who are contrite and humble. He continually refreshes them and even gives them new courage. How often do we need to be refreshed and have our courage renewed in order to face the challenges of everyday living?

The high and lofty one who inhabits eternity, the Holy One, says this: "I live in that high and holy place with those whose spirits are contrite and humble.

---

[1] 2016 Merriam-Webster, Incorporated

*I refresh the humble and give new
courage to those with repentant hearts.*
(Isaiah 57:15 NLT)

The story of Jesus and the Alabaster jar
has much significance with respect to
brokenness or humility. Jesus was anointed
for burial at Bethany in the House of Simon
the Leper.

*A woman came with an alabaster jar of
very expensive perfume, made of pure
nard. She broke the jar and poured the
perfume on his head.* (Mark 14:3 NIV)

The alabaster jar was of no use to the
Kingdom of God until it was broken, then the
good stuff was able to be poured out.
Sometimes we have to be broken before the
good stuff can come out. In our world, we
throw away broken things. In God's Kingdom,
when He finds something broken, He says
this is something He can use. He takes us and
fixes us and makes us stronger and more like
Him. Then He uses us for His glory.

A story is told of an Eastern village that through the centuries was known for its exquisite pottery. Especially striking were its high as tables, wide as chairs urns. They were admired around the globe for their strong form and delicate beauty. Legend has it that when each urn was apparently finished, there was one final step. The artist broke it and then put it back together with gold filigree. An ordinary urn was then transformed into a priceless work of art.

What seemed finished wasn't, until it was broken.

Out of Brokenness Comes Wisdom

When pride cometh, then cometh shame: but with the lowly is wisdom. (Proverbs 11:2 KJV)

Charles (Chuck) Colson, former special counsel to President Richard Nixon, is the author of twenty-three books, which have sold more than 5 million copies. He founded Prison Fellowship Ministries which has become one of the largest outreaches to prisoners, ex-prisoners, and crime victims.

Chuck Colson was a lawyer and his father was a lawyer. He had an Ivy League education. He turned down a scholarship to Harvard University and went to Brown University. He was known as Nixon's "Hatchet Man." He took care of Nixon's dirty work. In 1974 he pleaded guilty to Watergate-related offenses and served seven months in prison. In his book he stated his biggest problem was pride. He went from the White House to the Jail House. Chuck Colson was a man seeking power and success who finally found it in national disgrace and prison.

"Born Again" is the story of a man broken and transformed by the love and power of Jesus Christ. After the alabaster jar was broken, the good stuff came out. After Chuck Colson was broken, the good stuff came out (twenty-three books and a powerful Prison Ministry).

After we are broken, the good stuff comes out. When we are broken, we can say, like Paul, "It is no longer I who live, but Christ who lives within me" (Galatians 2:20 NKJV).

James 4:19 tells us, "Humble yourselves in the sight of the Lord, and He will lift you up. (NKJV). From this verse, we learn we have to do this for ourselves. This is not something God can do for us. We have to make a conscious choice to humble ourselves. So how do we get to this point that we are humble in spirit?

> *I humbled my soul with fasting.* (Psalm 35:13 KJV)

Fasting is one of the best ways to humble yourself. There is no such thing as a proud hungry man. Our politicians once believed in fasting and praying. The Governor of Texas recently proclaimed a day of prayer for rain since the state was going through a severe drought. After he had declared a day of prayer, he had a lawsuit filed against him for violating separation of church and state. This is amazing to me as I believe our country would probably not even be here if our forefathers had not fasted and prayed. Here are several instances of fasts proclaimed in America's history.

1) June 1, 1774, the House of Burgesses of Virginia, proclaimed a day of humiliation, fasting, and prayer when British Parliament ordered an embargo on the port of Boston. The diary of George Washington on June 1, 1774, reads, "Went to church and fasted all day."

2) May 9, 1798, President John Adams proclaimed a solemn day of humiliation, fasting, and prayer when this country was on the verge of a war with France.

3) June 12, 1815, James Madison, the fourth President, proclaimed a day of public humiliation, fasting, and prayer during the second War with Britain (War of 1812).

4) President Lincoln proclaimed three different days of humiliation, fasting, and prayer during the Civil War.

Fasting and prayer are major tools for the Woman of God and are needed to live a godly life in today's world.

We need to take a lesson from our forefathers and from the life of Mary and seek to humble ourselves in the sight of God.

Prayer: *Create in me a clean heart, O God, and renew a steadfast spirit within me. I call upon Your name, Lord, I **humble** myself as I seek Your face, and I ask You to show me what You have for me to do in Your name that I may humbly glorify You and bring advancement to Your Kingdom. In Jesus' name, I pray. Amen!*

Chapter 4

Phoebe the Deacon

I commend to you our sister Phoebe, a deacon of the church in Cenchreae. I ask you to receive her in the Lord in a way worthy of his people and to give her any help she may need from you, for she has been the benefactor of many people, including me. (Romans 16:1-2 NIV)

Phoebe was a leader and a deacon in the early church. Some Bible translations use the word "servant" and others use the word "deacon" or "deaconess." The Bible does not say much about her, but it is obvious Paul held her in high esteem. He says she helped him and many others. She is generally credited as carrying his letter to the Christians in Rome.

Phoebe was apparently a woman of wealth and influence who used her resources to help missionaries such as Paul.[2]

The word "deacon" essentially means servant with emphasis resting more on the person's character than any specific function. It was determined that a deacon must be "full of the Spirit and wisdom" (Acts 6:3). 1 Timothy 3:8-13 is the most complete account in Scripture addressing the office of deacon. "In the same way, deacons must be well respected and have integrity" (1 Timothy 3:8 NLT). Emphasis is placed upon the necessity of an exemplary life.

Deacons must be worthy of respect, sincere, not indulging excessively in wine, not pursuing dishonest gain, being found blameless, and a good manager of children and household. The reward for such service found is found in verse 13, having both an "excellent standing" and "great assurance" in the faith (before both God and people).

---

[2] NLT Study Bible, Tyndale House Publishers, Inc., Carol Stream, Illinois

These people are helpers in the practical areas of ministry, eligible to serve because of the unquestioned integrity of their lives.[3]

Prayer: *Heavenly Father, I ask You to help me to be worthy of respect, sincere, blameless, and a good manager of my children and household. Help me to be the leader I should be. Help me to have integrity and to live in truth. Teach me and guide me, in Jesus' name, I pray. Amen!*

[3] http://www.biblestudytools.com/dictionaries/bakers-evangelical-dictionary/deacon-deaconess.html

Chapter 5

Esther the Queen that Saved Her People

The King loved Esther more than all the other women, and she obtained grace and favor in his sight more than all the virgins; so he set the royal crown upon her head and made her queen instead of Vashti. (Esther 2:17, NKJV)

Esther was raised by her older cousin Mordecai. The 2nd chapter of Esther describes her as a lovely and beautiful young woman. After her mother and father died, Mordecai raised her as his own daughter.

According to the book of Esther, King Ahasuerus was over a very rich kingdom. He showed off the riches of his kingdom and the splendor of his majesty for one hundred eighty days which is six months. Then he wanted to show off his beautiful Queen Vashti, but she refused to come before him.

At the advice of his officials, he banned Queen Vashti started a search for another queen. Esther was very beautiful and obtained favor with the King. So, King Ahasuerus made Esther Queen.

Mordecai refused to bow before the evil Haman. Haman took revenge by ordering the execution of the Jews. Now, Esther risked her life by going before King Ahasuerus without being called, and she said if I perish, I perish. Esther was accepted by the King because of the favor she had with him. She was able to save the Jewish people because of her bravery. She risked her own life. The evil Haman was hanged on the gallows that he had made for Mordecai.

Prayer: *Heavenly Father, I come humbly before Your throne of grace and ask You to grant me the trait of bravery. Help me to be the strong but humble Woman of God I should be. Teach me and guide me, in Jesus' name, I pray. Amen!*

Chapter 6

Tabitha (Dorcas) Full of Good Works

At Joppa there was a certain disciple named Tabitha, which is translated Dorcas. This woman was full of good works and charitable deeds which she did. But it happened in those days that she became sick and died. When they had washed her, they laid her in an upper room. And since Lydda was near Joppa, and the disciples had heard Peter was there, they sent two men to him, imploring him not to delay in coming to them. Then Peter arose and went with them. When he had come, they brought him to the upper room. And all the widows stood by him weeping, showing the tunics and garments which Dorcas had made while she was with them. But Peter put them all out, and knelt down and prayed. And turning to the body he said, "Tabitha, arise." And she opened her eyes, and when she saw Peter she sat up.
Then he gave her his hand and lifted her up; and when he had called the saints and

widows, he presented her alive. And it became known throughout all Joppa, and many believed on the Lord. So it was that he stayed many days in Joppa with Simon, a tanner. (Acts 9:36-43, NKJV)

Tabitha, otherwise known as Dorcas, was a woman that was full of the good works and charitable deeds. She became sick and died. Peter went to her and raised her from the dead. Tabitha is an example of servanthood. She was well known for serving others. Why is serving others important, and what does the Bible say about servanthood?

Servanthood

When Jesus mentored His twelve disciples, they walked together for three years. Jesus taught and mentored by example and even sent His disciples out on their own in groups of two to experience the power of God for themselves.

These men served Jesus, grew into Men of God, and after His resurrection, they went on to change the world.

During their time together, Jesus taught them that the greatest ministry is about serving others without concern for themselves. In Matthew 20:25-28, Jesus called them to Himself and said, "You know that the rulers of the Gentiles lord it over them, and those who are great exercise authority over them. Yet it shall not be so among you; but whoever desires to become great among you, let him be your servant. And whoever desires to be first among you, let him be your slave— just as the Son of Man did not come to be served, but to serve, and to give His life a ransom for many" (NKJV).

When Peter bragged that the disciples had left everything and followed Jesus as if a "willing heart" was enough, Jesus told Peter he needed a servant's heart. "But many who are first, will be last; and the last, first" (Mark 10:31 NKJV).

Prayer: *Father God, show me how to serve you with a servant's heart that I may be used by You in building Your kingdom here on earth and become the Woman of God you want be to be. In Jesus' name, I pray!*

Chapter 7

Eve the Mother of All Living

And the Lord God said, "It is not good that man should be alone; I will make him a helper comparable to him." (Genesis 2:18, NKJV)

And the Lord God caused a deep sleep to fall on Adam, and he slept; and He took one of his ribs, and closed up the flesh in its place. Then the rib which the Lord God had taken from the man He made into a woman, and He brought her to the man. And Adam said; "This is now bone of my bones and flesh of my flesh; She shall be called Woman, because she was taken out of Man." Therefore a man shall leave his father and mother and be joined to his wife, and they shall become one flesh. And they were both naked, the man and his wife, and were not ashamed. (Genesis 2:21-25, NKJV)

***And Adam called his wife's name Eve,
because she was the mother of all living.***
(Genesis 3:20, NKJV, emphasis added)

Eve was the mother of all living. The first woman, the first wife, and the first mother. This started the concept of family, the institution of marriage and motherhood. People usually remember Eve negatively for being deceived by Satan in the Garden of Eden, but she contributed so much more on the positive side. She was Adam's helper and partner. She was the mother of all living. Wow! Who else can make such a statement. Adam stated Eve was bone of my bones and flesh of my flesh. "Therefore a man shall leave his father and mother and be joined to his wife, and they shall become one flesh".

Prayer: *Heavenly Father, I come humbly before Your throne of grace and ask You to help me be the best mother, wife, and leader that I can be. Help me to be the Woman of God I should be. Teach me and guide me, in Jesus' name, I pray. Amen!*

Conclusion

We can see the importance of women leaders in the Bible. They are strong, graceful, and cheerful and very important to God's kingdom work. However, people have long misconstrued the instructions Paul gave the Christians at Corinth in 1 Corinthians 14:34-35.

Let your women keep silent in the churches, for they are not permitted to speak; but they are to be submissive, as the law also says. And if they want to learn something, let them ask their own husbands at home; for it is shameful for women to speak in church. (1 Corinthians 14:34-35 NKJV)

Though relevant in the time of Paul and the problems faced by the early church, I believe this was a temporary rule for the culture and issues in the church at that time. The women leaders of the Bible contributed much to their time and ours.

There are many women of today who are contributing much as ministers, deacons, and teachers. God is using godly women like our biblical examples and those referenced from our modern world.

Prayer: *Heavenly Father, I come humbly before Your throne of grace and ask You to grant me wisdom and humility. Help me to be the Woman of God I should be. Help me to be a wise and humble leader. Teach me and guide me, in Jesus' name, I pray. Amen!*

Statement of Faith

I believe that one God exists in three persons: Father, Son, and Holy Spirit. Jesus Christ is the one and only Son of God who died for our sins and arose from the dead (1 Corinthians 15:1-8). The Bible is the inspired Word of God—a lamp unto our feet and a light unto our path (2 Timothy 3:16, Psalm 119:105). Every person has worth as a creation of God, but all have sinned and fallen short of the glory of God (Romans 3:23). Forgiveness of sins and the promise of eternal life are available to those who trust Christ as Savior and Lord (John 3:16). The church is the body of Christ on earth, empowered by the Holy Spirit, and it exists to save the lost and edify the saved (Ephesians 4:1-16). Jesus Christ will one day return to earth and reign forever as King of kings and Lord of lords (1 Thessalonians 4:13-18).

About the Author

 The author currently resides in Ransom Canyon, Texas. He has a Master of Science degree from Hardin-Simmons University and is a Family Nurse Practitioner. He has two children and two grandchildren. He attends a non-denominational church. He has been involved in two medical missionary trips to Honduras, two medical mission trips to Mexico, and a construction mission trip to Peru. He has also been involved in various Men's and Children's Ministries over the years.

Contact Info

To write the write the author, please E-mail him at: markmark_318@hotmail.com

Other Books by Mark Sundy

"MAN OF GOD: *Fulfilling Your Destiny as a Man*"

A Man of God is any man who delights in God's will and walks in the light of His truth, following in the footsteps of the Savior. This book will guide you in finding your own answers and becoming God's man!

"GOD's MAN KING DAVID: A Giant Print 40 Day Devotional"

God's Man, King David, was a mighty warrior, a great king, and a man after God's own heart. This powerful, 40-day devotional will help you learn from what David did right as well as from his mistakes.

"Dressed in Full Armor: A Powerful Praise Devotional Giving Glory to God"

We need to dress in the Full Armor of God to protect ourselves from the attacks of Satan. Isaiah 61:3 speaks of wearing a "garment of praise". This "garment of praise" could also be considered the "armor of praise". To dress in the full armor of God, you must put on your "garment of praise or armor of praise".

"Mom's Old Fashioned Holiday Recipes: A Christian Cookbook"

This book is a collection of my Mom's and Grandmother's recipes for the Holidays plus a few other recipes from family and friends. Each recipe in this book also contains a Bible verse mentioning God as our ultimate source of food. This book also includes tid-bits of cooking wisdom called wisdom pearls. Holiday recipes for Thanksgiving, Christmas, and New Year's Day are included . These are the Sundy Family Holiday Recipes.

"FULL ARMOR: A Powerful Praise Devotional"

A different version of "Dressed in Full Armor". This version is longer and has study questions.

All titles are available at Amazon.com online bookstore.

Printed in Great Britain
by Amazon

46765648R00036